SIMPLE WOOD JOINERY FOR BEGINNERS

EASY STEP-BY-STEP GUIDE WITH FUNDAMENTAL TECHNIQUES, TOOLS AND TIPS FOR JOINT MAKING

CLAYTON M. RINES

Disclaimer

The activities and information contained in this book is purely for educational activities only. The writer does not assert the accuracy or wholesomeness of any info gotten from this book. The views contained within the pages of this material are those of the author in its entirety. The author/writer will not be held accountable or liable for any missing information, omissions or errors, damages, injuries, or any losses that may occur from the use of information gotten from this book.

Bonus Book

Thanks for buying this amazing book. To appreciate your unending support, we are giving you a great book on Pour Painting that will bring forth your painter's instinct. You will derive unending hours of pleasure from practicing the beginner techniques you will learn from this book. Look out for invaluable periodic bonuses in your mailbox.

Download the book by clicking or typing the link below;

https://bit.ly/2LwTK4Q

Cheers,

Clayton M. Rines

Contents

"To dwellers in the wood, almost every species of wood has its voice as well as its features."

Thomas Hardy (Under the Greenwood Tree)

PREFACE

ou are looking for new materials, and simple ways of understanding wood joinery and your search have bought you here. There are several sub-disciplines of woodworking and joinery is one that requires patience and the urge to build a repertoire of skills that you would be proud of. The invaluable lessons and information-packed within this book will go a long way in making you a well-rounded individual in all aspects of your life and this chosen craft. Getting engaged in this timeless art with loved ones on weekends or during your spare time allows for time to bond, share ideas and build relationships. This art is all about the attention paid to details that will keep you engrossed for hours. In the end, it is time well spent as the results of your labor will last for years to come.

This book will guide you on developing wood joinery skills. You will get to understand and practice the basic techniques, tools, wood types needed to get you started.

Clayton M. Rines

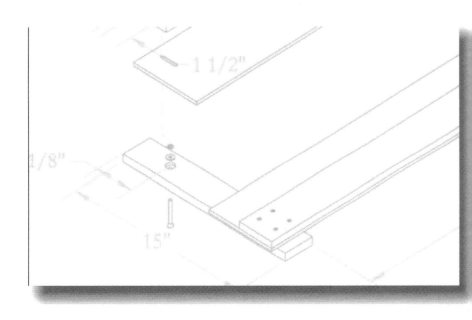

CHAPTER ONE

Wood Joinery is an art requiring a specific skill set from workers that need to be developed over time. Joinery is a subset of woodworking that is all about bringing well crafted simple pieces of wood together to create exquisite and highly intricate wood crafts. Wood joints can be formulated through the use of bindings, fasteners or the appropriate type of adhesives. The unique features of joints in wooden pieces such as the appearance, flexibility, sturdy nature are all factors of the individual materials used for the joint and the function of the joint itself. This gave rise to a variety of joinery methods to meet the ever diverse nature of woodworkers out there, e.g. the joinery requirements for a piece of table will most likely be different from that needed for the framework of a building.

Despite the fact that two pieces of wood can be joined together through the use of screws or nails, this does not give the durability and aesthetics that a finely finished work of art should have. Furniture making use of joints gives it immense value, and bringing a sense of satisfaction and accomplishment to both the owner and the woodworker.

The types of joints that are relatively known meet varying needs and the complexity and ease of construction, whether complex or straightforward all need some understanding of how wood joints functions.

Wood joinery is generally divided into those that do not make use of any form of fasteners (the traditional method) and the non-traditional methods are mainly composed of biscuit joints and domino joints that go a long way in improving the stability and looks of joints through simplicity and finesse.

The traditional wood joinery technique exploits the favorable inherent properties of woods to avoid the use of external materials. This form of joinery has through the years undergone slight modifications based on the culture and the areas where they are mostly used. Joinery in the Middle East and Asia employ several joints without any glues or nails as these materials are negatively affected by the environment and serve no useful purpose in the scheme of things. The woods found in these regions also contain large amounts of resins that do not agree with the use of glue.

One indicator of outstanding woodwork is the joints' firmness; you would need to derive accurate cuts. This would require a jig and a fence usage (essential woodworking tools); in guiding tools for dissection, the jig is employed, the cutting tools that might need to be guided include saw blades or router bits. The jigs see to it that different cuts are done with finesse, while the rigid, smooth tip on the power saw occasionally utilized to put the material that's being cut is known as the fence.

Indeed every wood has its peculiarities. We can even say woods are just like human beings, with attributes that make them very unique in their way. Some are even named based on those characteristics. These characteristics are taken into consideration when choosing any wood for woodwork projects.

Woods are classified into three using primarily the botanical composition of the trees they are lumbered from and the density. It is imperative to understand your wood's properties first to know the appropriate type of wood needed to get the desired result.

- Softwood
- Hardwood
- Engineered wood

Softwoods

Lumber and timber are softwood types derived from conifer trees. Gymnosperms are the biological name for conifers; just as their name implies, they reproduce cones and possess needle-like features. Examples of softwood trees employed in woodworking, craftsmanship, and cabinet making are Cedar, Fir, Redwood, Spruce, and Pine.

Hardwoods

Any tree type that doesn't produce either needles or cones produced by softwoods is known as hardwood. Deciduous trees are another name assigned to hardwoods, scientifically known as angiosperms. Hardwoods produce leaves and seeds. Oak, maple, cherry, mahogany, and walnut are species of hardwoods. Hardwood species are not always as strong as softwoods; varieties of species are famous for their alluring and exceptional wood grain patterns.

Some woods are also termed hardwoods, although they are not deciduous trees, e.g., the bamboo and palm. These plant types are scientifically known as monocotyledons because they share similar features with hardwoods, and they are often referred to as hardwoods. Bamboo and palm are seldom classified under engineered wood.

Engineered Wood

Engineered woods are the last type of timber you could come across. These wood types are most times manufactured because they can't be found in our immediate environment.

Treatment of engineered wood is often done through chemical or heat process. This is done to manufacture a particular wood product type that can meet specific sizes and unique features that nature can't provide.

Plywood, Oriented Strand Board, Medium Density Fiber Board, and Composite Board are examples of engineered wood. Wood veneers are, in some cases, taken to be a type of engineered wood since its manipulation needs to be done occasionally, and this could be carried out either through specialized techniques of cutting or building a grain pattern or a new wood through the combination of two different kinds of wood.

MOISTURE CONTENT AND MOVEMENT

Wood contracts and expands, and surprisingly this results in movements of the whole piece. The movement must be considered when embarking on any project; as the water content of the wood changes, wood moves. The wood of a tree that has just been felled is green, and its cavities are filled with sap. The sap makes up about 72% of the total wood moisture content, and this percentage varies in different wood types. The 28% left is made up of wood fibers, which saturates the wood's cell walls. A sponge increase in size when it is wet, and something similar happens to the wood fibers when they are placed in an environment with high moisture content.

Immediately the wood dries up; evaporation occurs then the trapped moisture/ water escapes. The structure and wood dimension remains constant until when water starts to escape, and then contraction sets in.

Approximately 4% to 11% of moisture content remains in the wood immediately after evaporation. The moisture content of wood is dependent on the environment. The amount of water found in the environment is somehow related to the water bound in the wood. They are directly proportional; that's, the rise in one leads to an increase in the other. On an average, wood tends to lose roughly 1% water content for every 5% drop in the environment's humidity.

Just as the wood's moisture is increased, the wood fiber increase in size, and as water is lost, the fiber tends to shrink. This leads to wood expansion and contraction, respectively. There's an increase and reduction of humidity in the environment in the northern hemisphere in winter and summer. Fireplace and air conditioning significantly have an immense effect on the relative humidity either indoors or outdoors. Also, there's humidity variation from a building to another if the internal temperature is different. Changes in location and season also have a great impact on the survival of woods.

DIRECTION OF MOVEMENT

We know that wood continually expands and contracts. But the wood movement in every direction isn't specific—the design of the grain permits movement in just three different directions.

Parallel to the wood grain, there's stability along the wood longitudinally. Green lumber reduction in size when it dries up is to about 0.01% of its original length; 3/32 inches is the highest movement carried out by an 8-foot longboard. Wood movement across the grains is tangential to the ring's growth, and about 8% length reduction is gone when treading this direction.

About a 4% extension is experienced in the radial direction from the pith across the tree's radius. Before this reason stated above, quarter sawn lumber has more stability than plain-sawn lumber. Tangential dissection is what plain-sawn wood undergoes. This tends to make its movement twice as much as the quarter-sawn lumber which undergoes radial dissection. However, the tangential movement is approximately 8%, while radial on the other side is approximately 4%.

CHAPTER TWO

HAND TOOLS

Hand tools are regarded as tool types that can be used by hand and don't require electrical power. It's more like a mechanical tool. These handy tools include hammers, cutters, clamps, and a lot more.

Types of Hand Tools and Usage

Hand tools are needed in our daily activities, and examples of such activities requiring hand tools include gardening, woodworking, and lots more.

A wide range of general-purpose hand tools or high-quality brands are readily available on the market. The use of hand tools is almost a must in most homes and workshops.

Some general-purpose hand tools are listed below:

✓ **Knives**

Kitchen knives are not what we mean here. Every household tool kit should possess a high-grade knife, which is for craft use. They are manufactured with rigid materials and can be utilized to open boxes, letters, or dissection of not so tough materials. For safety purposes, ensure the knife blade has a locking type of mechanism when it's not in use.

✓ **Scissors**

Scissors are found in almost every household for various functions. They have proven to be useful in practically all situations having to do with cutting, e.g., situations like a project at school, kitchen, DIY jobs, or anything you might need. It could also be used in getting seals or packages loose.

✓ Screwdrivers

This tool comes in various structures and sizes. It's one of the most common tools in our homes. Screwdrivers can bolt and tighten screws on surfaces, fastened hinges, installation of lamp holders and light switches in cabinet making. The screwdriver is made with varieties of blades with different widths designed for special functions. The blade is derived from carbon steel that's subjected to heat to enhance its strength. The handle can be constructed with a special plastic to ensure a firm grip.

✓ **Hammers**

This tool is crafted to deliver massive force on a small area. The tool comprises a wooden stick attached to a metal block. It can be used to fasten nails, breaking down objects into fragments, and also metal forging. This hand tool shouldn't be heavy, so its effect is fully exercised while securing nails on the wall. The hammer should be the appropriate size for the beholder for easy lifting and using the hammer without any form of discomfort.

✓ Wrench

To hold firmly and turn objects, wrenches are employed. They're instrumental in coupling woodwork or used in repairing bikes where it could be put to use to either loosen or tighten bolts or nuts, for plumbing where they're used for turning pipes. Varieties of wrenches are made by producers of hand tools to suit the diverse needs of woodworkers.

✓ Pliers

These are popular hand tools found in most homes, if not all. They are used in holding objects tight, removing bolts and screws, and also bend some materials. The material it most times bend, straightens, and even cut is the wire. Pliers with needle-nose tips and the ability to cut wires are the best type of pliers one could have. They are dual-purpose hand tools as they could be used in the home and also at workshops.

✓ Clamps

This is a device for fastening in holding objects firmly together to stop movement or separation through an inward application. This hand tool could be Adhoc because sometimes they are only used to hold woods in place while working on the wood; they could also be permanent, though. They are most time used to carry out repair jobs or assemble woodworks or DIY projects.

✓ **Chisel**

Chisels are one of the foremost commonly used tools in the history of woodworks. A chisel has a steel blade hooked up either to a picket or plastic handle. Chisel used with hammers and mallets are the tools mostly employed to separate, pare, and chop wood. Chisels most times are used mainly for developing joints of the woodwork and shaping wood.

Chisels are usually used on the surface of wood, utilizing paring cuts. Paring is the technique used to get rid of wood levels bit by bit when a slicing motion is employed. You might prefer to take away the wood by paring the surface utilizing hand pressure solely or taking away larger chunks by using intentional hits with the mallet or chisel hammer. This is usually based on how far the chisel goes into the wood, which may be adjusted by the angle the chisel makes to the wood's surface; the steeper the angle, the deeper the blade digs into the fibers.

You have to place confidence in the hand pressure for paring wood and use each hand to present the chisel to the wood. With the dominant hand on the handle and the alternative wrapped around or pressing the blade, push with a slicing motion into the wood.

Another use of chisel is split cutting. This can be wherever you have to position the edges for cutting on the wood's tip grain and hit the handle with a mallet. This pushes the chisel into the fibers on or with the grain to separate the wood away in chunks instead of shavings. This can be an excellent technique for quickly removing innumerable material, but you're restricted by the direction of the grain when it is not continuously straight or to your advantage.

Cut chopping can be cut directly into the grain, typically perpendicular to the grain, but not continuously. This can be a method used for chopping mortises and varied recesses. Using a hammer, if the chisel doesn't penetrate the wood, then you must contemplate presenting the chisel at another angle. This methodology works best with removing sections of the wood sections gradually.

Types of Chisels

There are many common sorts of chisels. The most well-liked kind is the bevel-edged type. This is often most suited for use in tool carpentry, but if you have got any of the following, they will get the work done but might not be as versatile:

- Firmer chisel
- Butt chisel
- Mortise chisel

POWER TOOLS

These are devices or machines powered by human power and the aid of an additional source of energy. These sources include pneumatics, electric motors powered using gasoline, internal combustion engines, and lots more.

When it comes to usage of power tools, its use should be restricted to specific environments, and caution should be taken when it is to be used within the home. Nonetheless, the tool that you would purchase should ideally come with specific functions, environments that it can be safely used in, and a host of other functions particular to the tool.

DIFFERENT TYPES OF POWER TOOLS AND THEIR USES

✓ **Air Compressor**

This power tool works with a fundamental principle; this principle involves converting power, which is stored in a pressurized air compressor, into energy needed for work. When you make use of the air compressor, it starts with air storage till it reaches its maximum capacity; this capability could vary depending on the air compressor you purchase because there are different models.

This power tool type is useful for spray painting, household and workshop cleaning, filling vehicle tires, and gas cylinders used for cooking. It is also used to charge some pneumatic tools, including nail guns, special types of hammers, and lots more.

✓ Trimmer

When you need to make your garden look stunning and fascinating, all you need for the job is a good trimmer. Trimmers use versatile monofilament lines rather than a regular blade. This can help cut grass, cut alternative objects close to the plant, and take care of irregular terrains. A trimmer uses gasoline, although currently, electrical motors trimmers are being sold in the market. The trimmer is usually used for cutting grass, giving the plant a pleasant structure and appearance at cutting an irregular piece of land. Also, you'll be able to use it for various farming cutting practices.

✓ Table Saw

Let's say you need crosscuts or need to saw any material; a table saw will be a beneficial type of power tool for you. Table saw comes with a sawing machine beneath a table with blades that permit you to move swiftly around everything placed on the table. The power of the table saw is generated from electrical motors; it can be simply shifted to the duty site for doing the cutting job because it comes with the transportable feature. It's helpful for deeper cutting that can't be handled with a saw or alternative power saws.

✓ **Drill**

You may have come to realize that this is the most helpful tool in our homes. Nowadays, there are many alternative varieties of drilling machines that you'll be able to make use of in accomplishing different jobs. Having a drill helps you in different ways, some of which are to hang up a painting on the wall, furniture creation, woodworks, metalwork, construction use, and lots more.

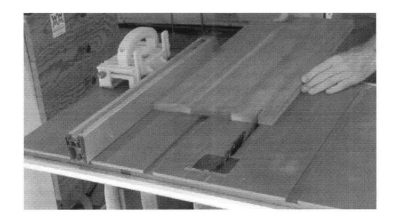

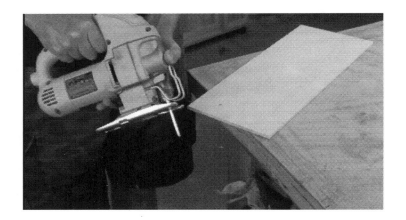

CHAPTER THREE

SIMPLE JOINERY

Simple joinery is a popular way of joining woods together. Under this topic, we would be discussing the following:

WOOD GRAIN AND STRENGTH

Technically, the word grain refers to the orientation of wood-cell fibers; that is quite different from the figure. It describes the distinctive pattern that regularly results from varied grain orientations. All grain varieties except straight grain could come as a blessing or a curse. As a result, wood with something aside from straight grain could also be sawn to supply typically exquisite figure; errant grain becomes a blessing. In structural applications, like home construction, lumber (mostly softwood) with straight grain loses some strength. And hardwood boards with the absence of straight grain need further care in machining to prevent tear-out and other unwanted reactions.

Why is the direction of wood grain vital during woodworking?

Wood is seen as a natural substance that's a lot stronger once the grain is continuous. Wood could be a natural or chemical compound. That is, it consists of parallel strands of polyose fibers held together by a polymer binder. Try lining up thousands of straws, all lined up and packed in a linear fashion. However, if one straw is weak, the others will make up for it by adding strength to the collection. In a situation where you split wood along the grain, you're breaking polymer bonds (easy); or when you break across the grain, you're snapping polyose fibers that are far more durable.

To get hold of the full advantage of a wood's strength:

- o Concentrate on the grain direction.
- o Continuously orientate along the grain to enable the fibers to support the load.
- o Whenever possible, cut the wood so that the grain is continuous, running the length of the board.

TYPES OF SIMPLE JOINERY

DADOS

Dado is a handy and powerful technique for connecting two stock pieces. Once you know how to chop a dado, you will notice these carpentry joints are incredibly helpful when building cupboards or bookshelves.

A dado may be a groove chopped in a wood piece so that another piece of wood can fit into the groove firmly. For example, when building a shelf 3/4" thick stock, one would cut a 3/4" wide groove into the acceptable dimension on the shelf and use adhesive to couple the shelf into the groove that was created.

TECHNIQUES FOR CUTTING DADOS

The methods used in creating a dado vary. The readily used technique is placing a stacked dado head cutter on a table mounted saw. This comprises a pair of 8 - 10" diameter, 1/8"-kerf saw blades with some 1/16" and 1/8" and chippers in between. Adding or removing chippers, you'll get just about any breadth groove between 1/4″ and 3/4″.

Dadoes that are way wider can be dissected by creating one or more passes through the saw. A type of dado cutter called a stacked dado head cutter can only be made use of on the table saw or preferably on some radial arm saws. Don't try using the stacked dado type on a round saw, as this process might be extremely hazardous.

An alternative to the stack dado set is the wobble dado set. This is just a saw blade positioned on a movable spindle. Setting the angle of the blade on the spindle will alter the dado width. This type is cheaper when compared to the stacked type. This set's outcomes are not predictable and based on what I have experienced; they are rarely acceptable.

I try so hard to prevent myself from purchasing a wobble type dado and save up my cash for the stacked type. I am also not comfortable with the dangers of employing the use of a wobble set.

CUTTING DADOES WITH A ROUTER

A well-known methodology for cutting dadoes is the use of a well-aligned dissecting bit on a router. When using a router for dissection of a dado, always have it in mind that you might want to reduce the speed of the bit a little and try fixing the shallowness for one or more pass to keep them from burning the material or bit.

Make use of a well-aligned edge for monitoring the guide. This makes sure a straight part is attained. Also, note that using a 3/4" router bit type will dissect a dado a little larger or more significant than a 3/4" plywood sheet. Although 23/32 bits types are readily in stock, employing 1/2" bit and a pair of passes provides the expected outcome.

EDGE JOINT

Edge to edge joint is a common joint type. It's most times used for coupling table tops of various lengths but the same thickness level, where biscuits joint types are employed across the board's planed edges.

For coupling a tabletop of different boards, display the boards side by side with every board's grain directed to the initial board's other direction. This will assist in maintaining the table top's stability during expansion or contraction.

The joints immediately attain a good position and use a pencil to inscribe marks along with every 4-6". This would represent the biscuits slots centerlines.

The next move is to carry out the board's separation and set the biscuit joiner for the accepted and acknowledged size of the biscuit joint. In this edge case scenario, a large number 20 size is most likely employed.

Setting the guide fence directly on the stock top, ensure alignment of the cutting guide with the mark inscribed with a pencil earlier on. Firmly hold the fence in position, begin to saw, and when the motor is at maximum speed, smoothly plunge the blade directly into the wood till pushing further until it is no longer possible. Then remove the blade altogether and repeat it at the next pencil mark.

Immediately after every slot has been dissected, a little adhesive should be added on every edge before inserting the biscuits. Apply a small quantity of glue into the other spaces directly on the edge, and then couple the boards together.

You might decide to hurriedly glue-up every edge of the tabletop and then combine the entire components. The clamps should be snuggled so that every space would be sealed completely. But also make sure you take caution to prevent squeezing too much to prevent the glue from spilling. If it spills, make sure you clean it off very well to avoid an unprofessional finish.

COOPERED JOINTS

Staved containers are produced in several sizes and styles, ranging from firkin to hogshead with barrels positioned in between. Coopers possess the most expansive plane of all. The 6/5 foot coopers jotter faces upwards, with an end of wood resting on the floor while the second end, which is on the other side, is elevated on a pair of legs. The Cooper operation is carried out using the eye, holding every stave at accurate bevels; when repetition on the other stave is carried out, it sums up to a great cask.

Each stave has similar angles, and the angle is 90 degrees. Before moving a stave to a jointer, the Cooper backs it using a drawknife to the case's contour. The stave back is just like a circle's segment; each edge's precise angle is right-angled to the circle's tangent, which has a constant angle of 90 degrees. No matter how broad the stave is, eyeballing a right angle of the circle's tip produces a unique stave. This process should be repeated several times to ensure perfection.

Cover work assigned to the joiner includes materials like porch columns and circular tips for chests. The process for joiners is the inverse of that utilized by coopers. You begin with regular stock; eggs should be beveled, adhesives should be added and round the exterior portion. The bevel of every edge is half of the angle found in between the stock faces.

A full-sized drawing should be made on the paper and derive the angles from the drawing, but if you prefer working scientifically, divide the circle with angle 360 by several staves as you would like to use.

With eight different staves, you would have 45 degrees each, so each stave would be required, a straight line to divert its paths to the circle. We are concerned with the internal angle; however, this 180 degree becomes 135 degrees after 45 degrees might have been subtracted, half of 135 is about 67.5 degrees. Any eight staves of similar length alongside edges which have underneath beveling at 67.5 degrees will give rise to a circle, or probably an octagon which can be easily reformed to a circle.

Once the angles must have been figured out, they must be placed precisely and continuously down at every edge. On the other hand, the square gives a fixed 90 degrees, although the sliding bevel could be set and locked at any particular angle you want. For a five-sided object, you should set at 54 degrees; the edges would be properly tested as the planes are being staved. The length of each starves requires equality, so you can't just continue carrying out the planning process if you make the angles way too steep. More often, you plane away excess mainly because where to stop wasn't visible.

RABBET

The rabbet is another common type that's dissected along the edge of a board rather than its center. You would regularly see it utilized for the coupling of edges to make them fit together firmly.

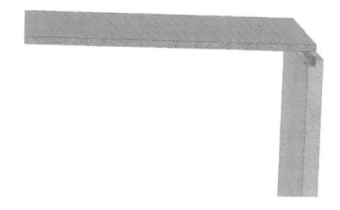

GROOVE

You might have worked with interlocking siding or wainscoting way back. If yes, then you should be able to recognize a tongue-and-groove wood joint. This is a wood joint type employed when you need to hold boards together on their edges, instead of across it ends; a particular end is bent with a protruding part called the tongue, and the other part is carved with a recession called the groove. They interlock firmly together.

This joint should be held firmly together with adhesives. Most times, the tongue and grove are dissected at an acute angle so that the woodworks must be combined with an angle and then sent down to ensure it is locked in place. It is less difficult to carry out this process using proper router bits. Hand planners are handy to carry out these processes. In woodworking, a groove could be a slot or trench dissected into a member that is aligned with the grain. The main difference between a groove and dado is that a dado runs across the grain while a groove aligns with it. Grooves are used for a range of purposes in cabinet making and other woodworking fields.

CHAPTER FOUR

THE MORTISE AND TENON JOINT

These joints have been employed in woodworks for ages by craftsmen all over the world, most especially when the joints to be connected have an angle of about 90°. These joints are sturdy and straightforward in their simplest forms, and they come in varying types that serve a multitude of functions. The simple and common form of mortise and tenon comprises a tenon tongue and a mortise hole. The tenon is crafted and is typically an extension of a rail, which is put into a cut in the shape you want on the other wood piece. The tenon should be a perfect fit for the mortise hole, and to ensure that it doesn't move or come apart, shoulders are put in place. In addition to the shoulders, other forms of substances or mechanisms can be used in securing the joint such as a wedge, pins, or glue. Other than in carpentry or woodworks, this joint type is also employed by blacksmiths and stonemasons.

MORTISE & TENON

Listed below are the other types of mortise that can be used in your projects;

Wedged half-dovetail mortise; it has a rear side having a large surface area compared to the front opening. There is an opening which permits the tenon access, but with the wedge in play, the tenon can't be removed once inserted.

Stub mortise; this form of mortise does not have much depth compared to other forms of mortises. It does not pass through the wooden piece and only goes in a fixed distance.

Through mortise; here, the mortise goes totally through the wooden piece.

Open mortise; it is open on the topmost part of the wood and typically has three sides.

Blind mortise; here, the tenon is fully inserted into the mortise and cannot be seen. You will find it in use in the construction of chairs and tables.

Tenons are extensions on pieces of woods that are inserted into openings called mortises. Typically, the length of the tenon is much more than its width. Tenons are of different types;

Through tenon; it goes through the hole and can be seen clearly on the other side.

Biscuit tenon; it's in the form of a biscuit.

Loose tenon; this type of tenon is independent of the joint to be worked on as it is not directly fixed to any main parts of the wooden pieces to be linked together.

Tusk tenon; here, a form of wedge device is used in securing the joint firmly.

Pegged tenon; it is also known as the pinned tenon, and a pin or peg is hammered into a hole on the mortise and tenon.

Stub tenon; the hole's size is factored in by how large or small the wood is. The mortise also has a larger width compared to the tenon, which prevents the tenon from showing.

It is relatively regular to have the size of the tenon and mortise proportional to the size of the wood. A good wood-crafting practice is to have the tenon have about 30% of the rail's width been worked upon.

MORTISE AND TENON EXERCISE

A mortise and tenon can be constructed with a router table, using the following steps;

1. The wood board to be joined are cut into the desired size; ensure that the end to be cut into the tenon is at a perfect right angle. Using your Try Square place the wood to be used as the tenon on the side of the wood to be used as the mortise and mark its length.

2. Mark three-quarters of an inch away from the top and bottom of the mark you made on the mortise board in step 2 above. That gives you the starting and stopping point of the mortise.

3. Measure one-third of the thickness of the mortise board on both sides and mark accordingly. That gives you the width of your mortise.

4. Load the router with the lowest straight tooth and cut through to make the mortise, taking note of the start and stop point initially marked in the step above. Cut gradually, starting with the lowest tooth on the router

and progressively increasing it till a one-inch mortise depth is achieved.

5. One-third of the thickness is marked for the tenon, and the wood is run over the quarter-inch router tooth on one side gradually until a one-inch depth is achieved. The wood is flipped over, and the same is repeated on the other side.

6. Test for fit and adjust accordingly.

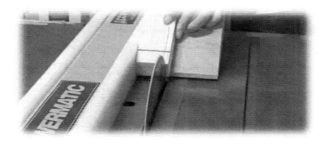

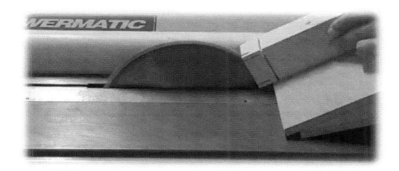

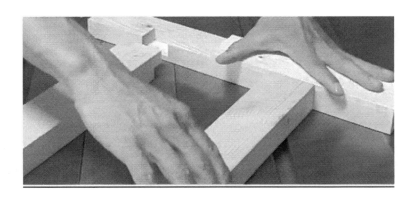

NOTE:

- ❖ The above measurement works for a relatively thin wood block. The measurements can be varied based on the thickness of the wood in use, and the weight the joint is meant to support.
- ❖ A hack for mortise and tenon construction makes the mortise first before making the tenon as a tenon can easily be fine-tuned to fit a mortise, but a mortise can hardly be adjusted to fit a tenon.

THE BRIDLE JOINT

There are a lot of similarities between the mortise and tenon joints with the bridle joint. At one extremity, the tenon is divided, and at the other end, the mortise is formed in such a way as to accept the tenon comfortably. With this joint, you will find a couple of adhesive varieties that will go a long way in giving support and prevent racking or any other undesirable actions. For more support, you can use pins or nails to ensure the joint's integrity is fully maintained.

CHAPTER FIVE

DISPLAY JOINTS

THE BUTTERFLY JOINT

This joint works perfectly for securing boards, or it can be used on boards that have already been joined but are experiencing some forms of problems with the joining method used. Besides securing boards, you can also find butterfly joints in use for decorations, structural and other functions. The butterfly joint most times is made of wood that is not the same as the main wood been worked on. A hole is formed on the wooden piece, and the butterfly joint is inserted in it, firmly securing both boards. They are also used to prevent crack movements and bring about the firmness of boards. Examples of projects using this type of joints are found in dahshur boats, Dutch tabletops in the 18th century, etc.

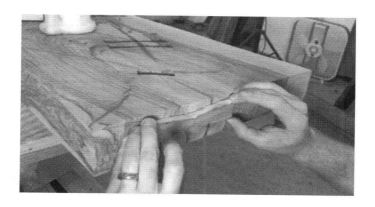

BEVEL TOP DOVETAILS

This joint is used to make it easy to join different pieces by softening the edges, bringing about a generally pleasing appearance and safety purposes. With woodworkers, this form of joinery is also used to form relatively small sizes that are not easily affected by environmental conditions.

PUZZLE SCARF JOINT

Finely fitting interlocking designs are formulated in two individual pieces, which are then brought together, the appropriate adhesives applied, and then firmly secured. The design that comes together to give the name to this joint type closely resembles when you bring your fingers together and lock them. The interlocking joint feature provides a large surface area for the application of the adhesive and hence a sturdy and robust joint. Do not confuse a box joint for a puzzle joint. You will find it in use for door constructions and floorboards.

CHAPTER SIX

DOVETAIL JOINERY

A true woodworker is known through dovetail joinery. These finger-like joint types are known for resilience and enable a firm, strong, and durable fit. These joints don't need a mechanical fastener, making them more suitable for furniture and other woodworks.

There are two different components of a dovetail joint; these components are tails and pins. The tails resemble a dove's tail while, on the other hand, on the opposite side of the board are features they try to fit in the middle of the tail to form a joint that can't be easily separated. Keep adding adhesives and coupling the joints firmly, and it would be impossible to separate.

Evidence shows that dovetail joints have been in existence for long and could be seen in antique shops. When you visit an antique shop, you could easily pull out drawers or other furniture and find out that most of the furniture is crafted with a dovetail joint.

Using a dovetail joint has numerous advantages, one of which is that it's the strongest of all joints, has a large adhesive area, is interlocking, resistant to separation, looks alluring, and doesn't necessarily need glue to be held together firmly.

Adverse effects of utilizing dovetail joints are that they might sometimes prove difficult to mark out and cut, and if they're constructed badly, these joints tend to lose all the benefits of using them that were stated above.

Project dependent, there are varieties of dovetail types to select for a project. Building the right type for your project will not only strengthen your skills but highlights your capabilities likewise.

The following are the different types of dovetail joints:

LAPPED DOVETAIL

There are different types of dovetail joints. The most common is a lapped dovetail. It is used to conceal a joint at one side but makes it seen on the other side. A very common application is in the construction of drawers. Here, the joint's mechanical strength is required to adequately fix the sides to the front of the drawer but still don't want the front to be seen when the drawer is closed.

It's a very tasking joint to dissect. It's quite similar to the through dovetail, except that the lap joint makes the waste accumulated a bit more difficult to get rid of completely from the pin member. To cut a laced dovetail, the following tools would be needed:

- Marking gauge
- Sliding bevel
- Marking template
- Dovetail saw
- Coping saw
- Scalpel or scriber
- Bevel-edge chisels

SLIDING DOVETAIL

As all woodworkers know, the sliding joint is very strong and dynamic in application, from case building to rail joinery. You have probably seen what a sliding dovetail looks like. It is a combination of a dado and the dovetail, with a dent on one side and a tongue on the other side. Since both dent walls are also called groove walls, and the tongue sides have angles like the dovetail, the joint's assembling has to be done by sliding the tongue into the groove side from an end.

The canted walls tend to give the sliding joint an upper hand over a dado. The joint resists tension mechanically; this means that the board on the tail can't leave the groove board. In the absence of adhesives, the parts remain linked. To separate the two parts, the wood must be crushed.

This feature of the joint makes assembly routines easier. You won't have parts destroyed while you are working with clamps. Your two hands are usually enough for assembling, even in the case of multi-part, just like a drawer chest. Panels that are slightly bowed can be drawn into line without bogus clamping configurations.

Another benefit gotten from the sliding dovetail is that it will permit the components to move without coming apart if left unglued. An example is a breadboard end. The application of slim wood strips across the end of a glued-up panel to hide its end grain allows it to remain flat. Leaving the joints unglued permits the expansion of the tabletop. Sliding dovetails are used to form extension table slides and join shelves to opposite bookcase sides.

BLIND DOVETAILS

Under blind dovetails, we have:

Half-blind dovetails

Woodworkers most times make use of a 'half-blind dovetail' when they want invisibility of the end grain from the front of the joinery. The tails firmly fit in mortises in the board end that is the front of the wood, hiding their ends.

Half-blind dovetails are most timed employed for drawer fronts and sides. This is a difference when compared to the practice of attaching fake fronts to drawers built with through dovetails.

HALF BLIND DOVETAIL

During the coupling of two wood pieces, the most popular joint to be employed is the through dovetail. The through dovetails are durable and fascinating, but there are still some situations where this dovetail joint isn't the most suitable.

For example, during the joinery of a drawer side to the drawer front, one wouldn't prefer making use of a through dovetail joint, as the tail ends tend to show through the drawer front.

In this scenario, the most acceptable dovetail joint type to be employed is the half-blind dovetail.

The half-blind dovetail is very precise; just as it is called, a section of this joint can be seen while the other is concealed. This joint is rigid as the through dovetail but is utilized in scenarios like the drawer front scenario discussed earlier.

Creating Half Blind Dovetails

The local method of building half-blind dovetails doesn't show much difference from the methodology of through dovetails creation, but there are few points to keep in mind:

The portion that isn't to be cut is called the lap. The lap positioned on the board should have a thickness not less than 1/8", yet should not, in any case, have a thickness of more than 1/3 of the pin board's thickness; this is to maintain the dovetail's strength.

MITRED BLIND DOVETAIL

This joint can also be referred to as the full-blind mitered dovetail or the full blind dovetail, and it is commonly used in exquisite woodworks and cabinet construction. The exterior part of this joint is formed so that it is not observed by looking closely at it. The joint is designed so that only the interior part meeting at an angle of 45° can be seen on close inspection.

Tips for cutting dovetails

1. Cut the woodblocks to be joined to the same size and ensure the ends are square. Check for square-ness using your Try square.

2. Sand the surfaces you want facing inside and mark accordingly. The use of a marking gauge here would be helpful.

3. Set the marking gauge to the woodblocks' thickness and mark a line around the ends you want to join together, marking the front, back, and the two edges. It helps if the gauge is set a little more than the thickness, at most 1/32. This makes for a little extension of the pins and tails above the woodblock. When finished and glued, this extension gives room for a little sanding to give a perfectly shaped corner.

4. Decide the woodblock where the pins would be cut from. Generally, it's easier to cut out the pins first. In deciding which woodblock holds the pin, always remember that corners with dovetail can be pulled apart from only one side. To ensure the cut is against the direction of pull. A good example is a drawer; the pins should be on the front block and tails on the side; this way, you are sure the joint would still hold no matter the pull.

5. The next step is to determine the size of the pins you intend to use. Pins are generally about half the size of tails. This is subject to change. When determining pins

and tails' sizes, note that large tails produce weakened joints, the same for too narrow tails.

6. Next, secure the wood block in a vice and saw the tail with the backsaw, following the markings made in step 3 above.

7. Use the chisel to clean up the edges of the tail till they are flat and crisp. Do not chisel in a vise; clamp over a flat surface instead.

8. Set the pins on the woodblock where the tails would be cut. Taking note of the previously marked gauging line and marking around the pins. The woodblock mustn't shift at this point.

9. Saw through the lines and clean with the chisel as done in step 7 above.

10. Join the pin and the tail with a gentle tap to assess the fit. If it is too loose, the joint won't hold. If it is too tight, it will result in splitting.

11. After the fit is assessed and seen to be perfect, glue accordingly and rejoin.

12. Sand the edges of the joint for a smooth finish.

Note: Two woodblocks with varying thickness can be joined, but when this is done, two different marking gauge settings are needed, one for each thickness of woodblock you intend to join.

BANDSAW IN DOVETAIL CONSTRUCTION

The bandsaw is a friendly piece of woodworking tool used in the cutting of curves, crosscut short pieces, the formation of cabriole legs, etc. However, this tool is favored in the cutting of shapes that are irregularly shaped, ripping lumber into thinner and manageable sizes, provision of smooth cuts, etc.

A regular bandsaw is mostly made up of wheels, which can either be two or three, which are the mechanism for securing the cutting blade in position. There is also a support framework, which can be in the form of a bench or table which should be sturdy and stable enough for everyday work. Bandsaws come in varying sizes, from the standalone floor models to the tabletop types.

The benchtop types are easy to carry around and could be stationed on a flat surface or secured firmly on an appropriate surface to give some support. The benchtop types do not have the robust powers associated with the floor models, though they are far cheaper to buy. The size of a bandsaw goes a long way in determining the project's size that you can embark upon. There are two main measurement types; the length between the saw's throat and the interior blade edge tip is one form of measurement, e.g., if there is a distance of fourteen inches in between these two points, it can handle stocks of lengths between ten inches and twenty-four inches. The other type of measurement is the depth of the cut made by the blade. If the blade can cut six inches deep, you can typically cut between five to eight inches with the same blade.

In addition to the features mentioned earlier, the type of blade and size of the table used is important. Smaller tables won't' give you the required real estate to move the blade around with ease. Angle 45° is the main angle for working, and with a large table, you should be able to get this done, especially when incorporated onto a lathe. You will find a miter gauge for crosscut cutting and a fence that enables resawing with your band saw.

Band saws also possess a tension guide to match the blade length's tension.
The blade guides could be alternated up and down to match the stock's hardness or toughness, which is being dissected.
Resawing is one of the most difficult sawing activities or sawing hard stock into a much thinner stock. This is occasionally employed when highly figured wood is picked for

a door panel or cabinet project. Wide blades must be utilized. The guidelines for the saw must be followed properly to prevent the blade from wandering or "running out." A fence must also be in place. Despite all these, some mistakes tend to occur; the blade tends to saw from one side to another. For example, a Jet saw has a resaw guide that gets fixed to the saw fence and eliminates or reduces the lead problem. A high fence can also be derived from wood stock and coupled to the saw table.

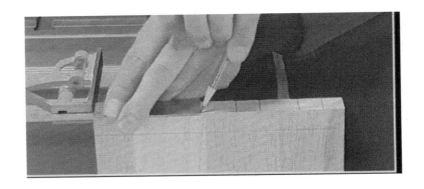

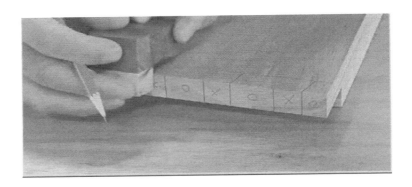

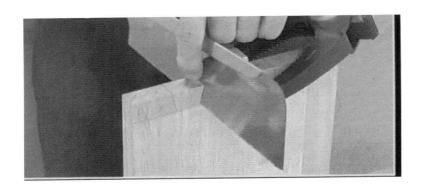

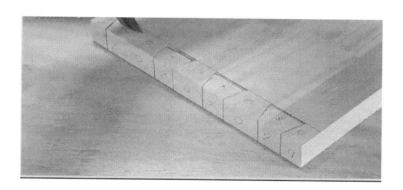

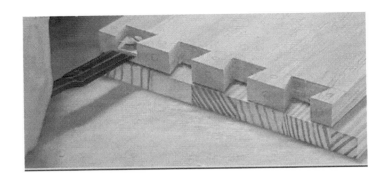

SCARF DOVETAIL CONSTRUCTION

Mark the centre on four faces

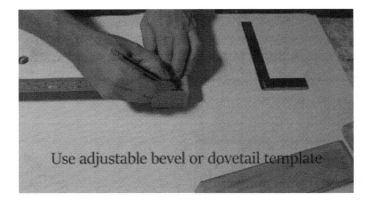

Use adjustable bevel or dovetail template

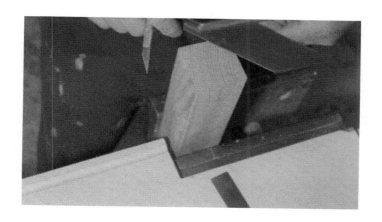

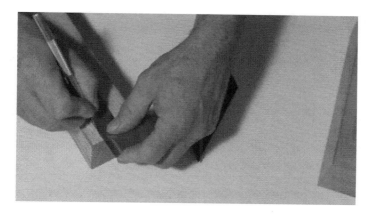

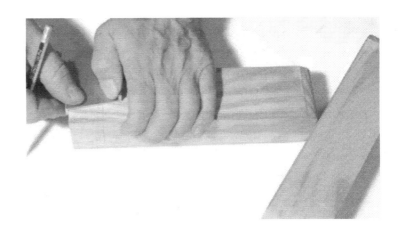

Mark Waste - Important as join get more complicated

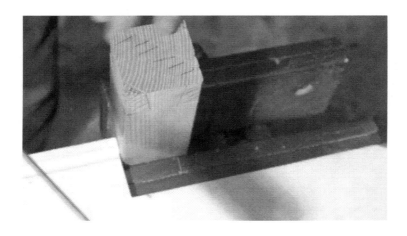

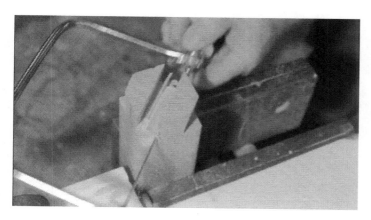

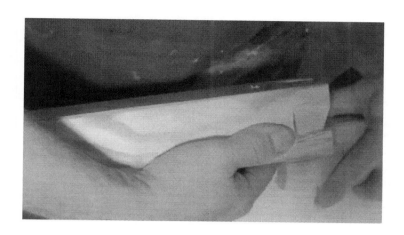

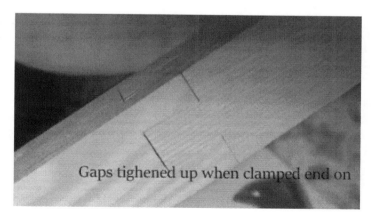

Gaps tighened up when clamped end on

CHAPTER SEVEN

STRAIGHT-LINE JOINTS

RUBBED JOINT

Just as sprung joints are very good for coupling two-edged board firmly together to create a panel, they are devastating for non clamped rubbed joints.

A strong emphasis has been dedicated to sprung joints; several works have been written and established stressing such a joint's advantages. While I support their claim, at times, what is glaring tends to elude us. We continue applying a certain type of technique that has been drummed into our heads by a hypnotic claim through the opinion of others, which would lead to disastrous outcomes if we were to make use of a similar technique, but this time a different application. I feel these constraints need not be skipped but noted in any future projects to be embarked upon.

A rubbed joint's success consists of only two major things, adhesive and two straight, no gapped edges. A sprung joint possesses a second hollow right in the center; producing a great rubbed joint would be impossible. The other point is the adhesive type that's best for a rubbed joint is hide glue. Yes, you could do away with tiny pieces using ordinary PVA or other fast-setting PVA glue, but for a little cabinet or table or even a coffee table, only a type of glue called the hide glue would suitable for such an application, i.e., rubbed joint. Hide glue alone can draw two coupled edges together as it dries, leading to the formation of a good solid joint, and for that to happen, there have to be no gaps.

SCREW JOINT

The screwed butt joint makes use of screws inputted immediately after the joint has been coupled together. These screws are often inputted into the tip of wood or on the long grain side of a member and elongated through the joint down to the corresponding member's end grain. Owing to this fact, long screws are needed to make sure excellent traction is attained. These joints may undergo joinery; it is not necessary, though.

In solid timber woodwork, it is very usual to bore a hole in the frame; this is done to hide the screw head. This also permits a larger portion of the screw's body to penetrate the corresponding member for greater traction. After driving the screw into the joint, the counterbore can be filled with a moderate and fitted piece of dowel from an offcut of similar wood, making use of a cutter for the plug.

Some systems are readily available for screwed butt joints, and there's provision for a plastic cap to be fixed firmly to the screw head after it must have been driven back in. Counterbores are not needed for these types of fasteners. This mode of operation is most peculiar to manufactured board products.

This joint type is common in both the carcase and frame joinery. Modular kitchens make steady use of this fixing method.

Some uses of screw joints include:

Frame joinery (e.g., face frames, web frames, door frames)

Cabinet carcase building (carcase sides to top and bottom, fixed shelving/partitions).

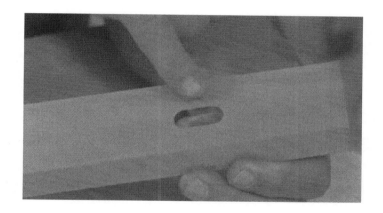

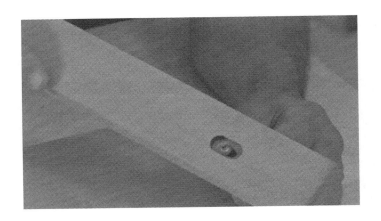

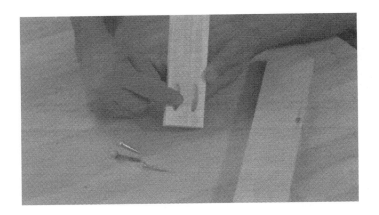

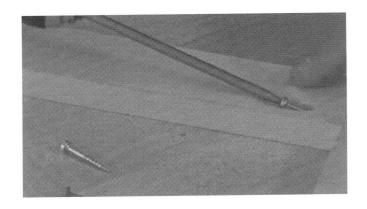

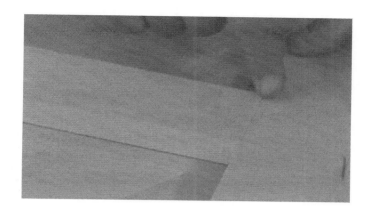

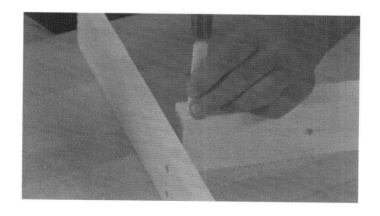

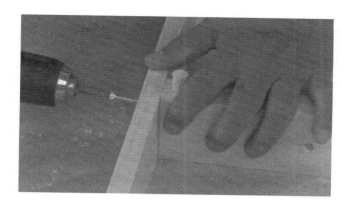

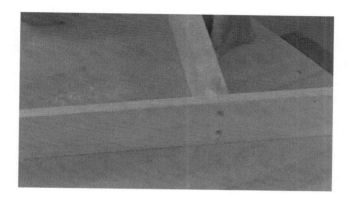

SPLINE JOINTS

A spline joint is formed when a wooden spline is inputted and coupled firmly into a slot that has been cut in a different woodworking joint, which is most times usually a butt or mitered joint.

The spline is put in place to reinforce the joint and assist in maintaining the alignment of sections with each other. This little enhancement gives considerable strength to whatever kind of joint it's used for.

Spline could be derived from plywood, hardwood, or similar material, with the joint being, strengthened. For strength, the grain of natural woods should be designed so that it's running along the joint in the work piece.

You shouldn't force splines into grooves, which could cause distortion or splitting. Rather, they should slide in without stress and absence of any side play to give room for adhesives to make a solid joint.

When utilized between two different boards, either miter or edge joint, the length of the spline should be a bit less than the length of the two slots to ascertain that the joint close well.

MITER SPLINE

The miter spline is very good for reinforcement of picture frames and even cabinet face frames that use mitered corners. Little decorative boxes can use dissimilar colored splines with mitered edges for visual effect, likewise reinforcement of the joinery.

Miter spline joints look fascinating when using dissimilar wood colors. A bright-colored spline set in a dark wood will highlight the joint. A dark walnut spline placed in a brighter colored wood would most likely do something similar.

EDGE SPLINE

These splines are occasionally used in making bigger and wider panels out of many narrower boards. An edge to edge glue up already has strength due to the long grain to long grain surfaces; splines give extra support, likewise assisting in the joint's alignment.

The most popular edge spline joint has the groove and spline spanning the full length of the boards. The spline is very obvious when the joint is sighted from the tips.

If the looks are not imperative, plywood is a superb spline for this job. The spline can be derived from hardwood for contrast.

The halted edge spline is like a halted dado joint in that the groove is stopped short of the board end, but this happens on both ends in this scenario.

They are utilized for the edge of hardwood furniture like tables, where the woodworker would prefer additional capability from the spline, but in the absence of visibility.

Although the groove can be cut on the table saw, it is probably easier and less work to rout it out on a router table with a slotting bit.

The slot corners can undergo chiseling to get a square shape to comfortably take the spline, or its ends could be smoothened into a fine circular shape using a sander.

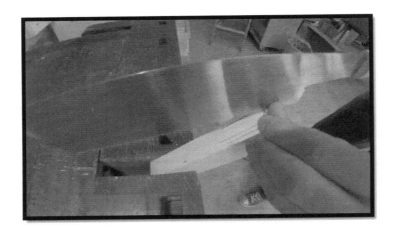

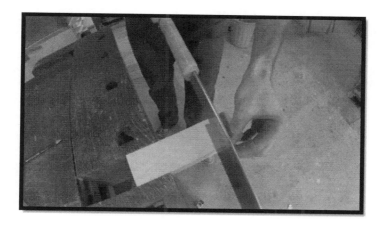

EDGE JOINT

Making a perfect edge joint is a compulsory task for all cabinet makers who realize that boards come in minute sizes nowadays.

In a perfect world, if a 36" broad cherry board is required for the edge of your dining table, you might visit the lumberyard and choose from a stack of 36" broad cherry boards, all derived from trees with measurement of 60"-70" in diameter. Although in this world, if you request a yard hand at the closest lumberyard to you, where they preserve 36" broad cherry boards — well, I can only assume the response you might receive.

Many years back, when I required an 18" broad cherry boards to give Queen Anne highboy, I encountered difficulties trying to find nice 10" boards that could easily be glued up in pairs. And occasionally, we find ourselves gluing up panels with measurement of only 8 - 10" from tiny stock. This depicts adequately the constantly changing nature of hardwood in American forests. Rather than taking mature trees with diameters of approximately 40" or more as their predecessors carried out, many woodworkers make use of smaller specimens. This turns into the edge joint, making it the most paramount woodworking joints for every cabinet maker.

Sometimes edge joints are supported with cross-grained splines or even biscuit joints. This assists with alignment, although they do give some strength and a moderate area of glue surface. Edge joints are also sometimes produced, making use of tongue-and-groove cutting style. This process is occasionally utilized for joints that are not glued, for example, when you are butting together stock for a floor or a cabinet.

The cabinetmaker makes use of a basic butt joint glued together with very good glue. When built, butt joints are very strong, sometimes heavier, and bigger than the wood adjacent to the point of joinery.

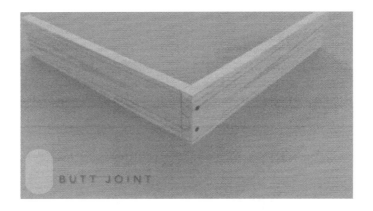

BUILDING THE JOINT WITH THE AID OF A MACHINE

One of the easiest things you could carry out to alleviate your edge joints' status is to access the tables of your jointer for adequate alignment. Reduce the infeed table's height till its top surface is 1/8" lower than the table above. Lay a wide straight edge along both tables. Its bottom edge should depend on the surface of the table above and sit 1/8" above the surface of the table below.

Do a proper check to see if there is a constant 1/8" gap between the straight edge base and infeed table's surface across its total length. You should also do a proper check to ensure that there is a constant 1/8" gap across the length of the table. If there is any change detected, make sure you check the owner's manual for details on how to go about rectifying the glitch.

This kind of check should be carried out only once or twice yearly. However, you should occasionally run this check using a Try Square to experience that the fence is 90° from the tables.

Before an edge can be joined, you must first create a plane for reference on a corresponding surface of the board that's about to undergo joinery. At a minimum, a side of the board that's being jointed must be leveled. This can be carried out on your joinery machine if its head used for cutting is broad enough. If it isn't, you should try flattening a reference plane placed on your board with hand planes and some winding sticks. Or you carry out what I occasionally do with broad boards: cut them in two halves to be coupled after both halves must have been straightened and displayed on my 6" jointer.

Sadly, you can't carry outboard straightening with a thickness planer due to the relative small size of the table. This tool makes a particular area of the board sleek and ensures parallelism to the other surface. If the reference surface slides frequently, the thickness planer will ensure the other surface's smoothness while hoarding the ripples.

Since you can edge joint a stock that possesses just a face flattened (the one you're going to press against the fence), having two straight, sleek, parallel surfaces gives more options when feeding stock along the jointer. So I strongly advise flattening the opposing side on the thickness planer. It is not compulsory at this period to bring the board way down to the final thickness level.

CHAPTER EIGHT

MACHINED JOINTS

SCARF JOINTS

Scarf joints have been utilized in the construction of wooden boats for years now. There are many variations on this joint type; some of these variations include feathered, tabbed, and hooked scarves. And there are many applications for them, from bringing together planks to the creation of maximum length most staves from very short pieces.

With the improvement in structural engineering, which gave rise to less heavy boats—coupled with important progress in glues—scarf joints' mechanical features and capacity when compared or related with solid timber must be well comprehended.

Scarves are described by the length of slopes about the pieces' hardness coupled together; this relationship is termed a simple ratio.

Below are some examples of scarf joint application;

Bevel-cut scarf joints

By dissecting ends of an angle, you get to expose additional long grain for stronger bonds. The less blunt the angle, the bigger and better the gluing surface. For instance, a 45° bevel appreciates the gluing surface by 40 percent and aids in hiding the joint line on a neatly profiled surface. To get in line with the angles, slice one end on the side of the saw blade and the mating end on the other part. If your blade bevel angle changes from 45°, the pieces will still end up mating.

Miter-cut scarf joints

Try this joint for an even wider and bigger gluing surface. Start by creating a 4:1 angle guide that's larger than twice the width of the work pieces. Similar cleats on both ends of the triangle aid positioning on the face of the two work pieces. Angles on the two work pieces should be marked and bandsaw the samples to within 1/32" of the scrap sides' lines.

The slip joint is a large, sleek, machine-cut joint for little batch jobs like the corners of wood frames. The slip joint has similar basic geometry on its face or surface, just like a traditional bridle joint, but it is created in a very outstanding way. Its large, slim proportions tend to provide a very large gluing area.

SLIP JOINT

With the help of the bandsaw and with some prepping, the capability of making several similar perfect fitting slip joints becomes a possibility for everyone. Once a joint fits perfectly, everything else is pretty elementary.

The major use of a slip joint is for low profile frames corners. Frames require nice stable wood that will neither twist nor bow when there is a change in the moisture content level. You might prepare your wood with basic hand tools or machines, but if you utilize an electric planning machine, it's best to round off with a hand plane after. Work with the grain to get rid of any ripples on the surface.

Be prepared to carry a little hypothesis at first - the secret of creating well-fitted slip joints is in the shims' hardness. Once the shims are in good condition, maintain this condition, and every slip joints you work with after will fit perfectly well.

BISCUIT JOINTS

This joint is a reinforced butt joint that has an oval-shape. A biscuit is made of dried and well-compacted wood like the beech utilized in the two pieces of wood matching mortises and tenons. Well, almost everyone makes use of a biscuit joiner when building matching mortises in situations where accuracy is not imperative. This joint is created to permit flexibility in glue-up.

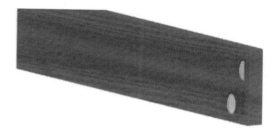

BISCUIT JOINT

SCRIBED JOINT

The ascribed joint is put to use were two different moldings confluence at an interior corner. Instead of being mitered, the end of a piece is designed to fit the profile of the other piece.

This joint type is also regarded as coping joints, and coping saws were developed for this purpose. Usage of the scribed joint is during fitting skirting boards; for instance, it is best practice to use a scribed joint for every interior corrosion angles and another type of joint called the miter joint for the exterior angles. This is because wood might shrink along its width, and this would make the miter joint open up in the interior, which is not a desirable effect.

CHAPTER NINE

SPECIAL JOINT

CHINESE CHAIR JOINT

Chinese furniture has been in existence for a long time. Lacquer furniture has been in existence in the Han dynasty tombs as early as 206 B.C. And during the era of the Southern and Northern Dynasties from (420-589), with the influence of the Buddhists, the Chinese commenced evolving the habit of sitting on the low platforms or sitting with feet pendent on furniture like chairs and stool.

There is extravagance in the mortise and tenon technology and its sturdiness, seamlessness, and strong building of wood joints. Although it is a stylish and classy approach, and its longevity is one of the major reason why a lot of woodworkers still make use of it till now. It is not new as Chinese Architects have put mortise and tenon joinery into for house construction and other woodwork for a long time now. That is why this style has been put to use up to this present day, mainly because of its reliability and relative ease of construction. Without the utilization of any materials for fastening, the strength remains constant throughout its lifetime.

Truly indeed, while it is true that varieties of Chinese dynasties have undergone implementation and distributed a lot in terms of building design, Chinese joinery is still constant. It has been a tested formula and a home name for cabinet makers. So, if furniture from China comes your way, its sturdiness and strength would be evident. Mortise and tenon technique is much appreciated in China because it's a rare and simple joinery type.

CORNICE JOINT

Cornice, coving, and architrave are terms that are often used the wrong way or used as though they were synonymous.

A cornice is a molding utilized to hide the joint found between a ceiling and a wall, so this ensures that it doesn't have to be finished, and any form of cracks or irregularity is concealed.

A cornice can either be plain or heavily fashioned.

Plain cornice maybe sometimes called 'coving.'

Cornice and coving comprise plaster, paper-covered plaster, polyurethane, and a few others.

An architrave is a form of molding that's positioned above a door, window, or any other form of opening; in this case, the architrave extends along the side moldings top to the opening. Nonetheless, the term architrave is mostly used to describe or address any horizontal or upright moldings that create the framework to a door, window, or other openings in the building industry. An architrave is often derived from timber.

GREEN WOODWORKING JOINT

Another form of woodcraft is Green woodworking or, in other words, carpentry; this is all about converting unseasoned or green timber into finished forms or furniture. Unseasoned wood is a wood type that has just been felled or preserved by keeping it in a water-filled trough for maintenance of its naturally increased water content. Green wood is quite softer compared with seasoned timber, and it's quite easier to shape when using hand tools. As the unseasoned wood loses its moisture content, shrinkage happens, and the green woodworker can use this shrinkage to ascertain very tight joints in their business. To increase the shrinkage effect, one half of a joint may be over-dried in a kiln while its other component is left green. The constituents tighten against one another as the parts swap moisture with the immediate environment. Swelling of the dry tenon inside the shrinking "green" mortise creates a very firm, tight, and permanent joint even though adhesives are not available. Another traditional green woodworking job is bodging, where chair constituents were created directly from the woods and transported to workshops where the chairs were joined together by cabinet makers. Green woodworking has experienced a recent revival because of its high media influence and the hand tool woodworking revolution.

OTHER BOOKS BY THE AUTHOR

The Pyrography Beginners Workbook with Exercises

Learn to Burn with Step-by-Step Instructions with Introduction to Basic Tools, Techniques, Modern Wood Burning Textures and Patterns, and Sample Project Ideas

The art of pyrography, also known as pur graphos (fire writing), is as old as mankind, and this form of art gives immeasurable satisfaction to artists by giving power to the imagination. This book opens up a brand new vista to you, laying bare all you require to begin your journey with this timeless art. In The Pyrography Beginners Workbook with Exercises, Clayton M. Rines shows you the basics of writing with fire, types of tips, pens, shading techniques, and other lesser-known methods that help you develop your craft. You would learn the in and outs of buying your first pyrography machine, types of woods to burn, safety tips, maintaining the workroom, and other essential tips for successful wood burning projects. This book offers you some easy to carry out projects as a way of getting you accustomed to the art of wood burning, from making of wall clocks, key holders to creating cup coasters and bangles with images.

You will learn;

- Easy projects for everyone
- Learn how to write, shade and apply outlines
- The importance of temperature settings
- Knowing what type of burning nibs to use
- Important safety tips
- Must know techniques for texturing and finishing
- Burn those great gifts for your loved ones
- And so much more!

With The Pyrography Beginners Workbook with Exercises, you are on your way to becoming a pro in wood burning carvings, wooden plates, household items, and so much more. Grab a copy today and begin your pyrography journey.

https://www.amazon.com/dp/1674755775

A Guide to Wood Finishing for Beginners: A Step-by-Step Manual on How to Finish, Refinish, Restore, Stain, Dye and Care for your Furniture

This is the ultimate wood finishing guide for an exquisite project.

Applying a well-thought-out and researched finish can bring out the beauty and shine in an otherwise bland work. On the flip side, a well-built and alluring piece of woodwork can be turned into an ugly duckling with a lousy finish.

Clayton M. Rines takes you on a journey through one of the aspects of woodworking that many crafters will rather avoid. He removes the cloud of mystery surrounding wood finishing. You will navigate the minefield of finish application, refinishing, and staining with ease like a pro. You will discover new and existing methods that work on how to select the best type of finish for your project, correct errors, prepare the wooden surface, and troubleshoot.

As a beginner or a pro, it is pertinent that you understand the basics of staining, coloring, and dyeing your wood. This will give you a wide array of options to play within any project, thus breaking down restrictions that might have been in place. When you fully understand the foundation of wood finishing, you will be able to bring out the hidden beauty of your wood, promote its longevity, and make the whole wood-crafting process a seamless experience.

"A Guide to Wood Finishing for Beginners" is packed with invaluable tips and hints that will enlighten you on the reasons why you should go through the process of finely finishing your wood, the methods to embrace, and what to avoid.

You will learn the following and much more ;

- Simple and safe method of applying spray finish

- The different types of solvents, oils, and varnish

- The types of wood and how to apply finish to them

- Stripping and Refinishing

- Stain and dye application

- Restoring furniture

- Water-based and oil-based finishes

- An easy to understand approach to the subject theme

- The beginners guide on polishing, spraying, sanding, etc

- Fixing mistakes

- Troubleshooting

Written with you in mind to help solve your wood finishing fears as a beginner or an experienced hand needing a bit of refresher, this is a must-get book.

CLICK on the BUY button to begin finishing your wood with style today.

https://www.amazon.com/dp/B08LPJ6C9Z

The Simple Woodcarving Book for Beginners: Simple Techniques for Relief Carving, Easy Step-by-Step Beginner-Friendly Projects, and Patterns with Photographs

Getting started with woodcarving or any other form of art can be a bit daunting. You are at a loss on the type of equipment and tools to purchase the simple projects that your skill level can start with. Mr. Clayon M. Rines has got you all covered with everything to get you started as a novice woodcarver or an experienced hand looking to refresh your wealth of knowledge.

The Simple Woodcarving Book for Beginners, Simple Techniques for Relief Carving, Easy Step-by-Step Beginner-Friendly Projects and Patterns with photographs is a personal guide with a passionate teacher. You will learn how to make those clean cuts in different ways, sharpening your tools and putting the finishing touches on your work.

Your desire to master this age-long art of woodcarving has brought you this far, and this passion will be fueled and guided with everything you will be learning from the pages of this book. Clayton M. Rines will expose you to secrets of the trade, such as the basic cuts, smoothening techniques, how to carve contours, and the essentials or relief carving.

The directions to follow for each method are clearly explained and accompanied by photographs to further breakdown the process. What do you need to get that first project done? This book in your hands, a few well-honed essential cutting tools and a piece of softwood, and you will be on your way to carving the most amazing and exquisite objects that will continuously recharge your bank account, serve as gift items to friends and loved ones and give you joy unlimited. With your desire to fully understand everything about carving in relief and producing masterpieces, this all-encompassing book on woodcarving will enlighten you and show you the best way to go about it.

From when the idea comes to you, the initial cut to the final finishing touches, these steps will guide you every step of the way; •Step-by-Step practice projects with visual guides to build your confidence levels• Types of woods, tools and your workspace, finishing •Basic and well-explained carving techniques• Detailed directions• Carving relief projects• Maintaining and keeping your tools well-honed and in perfect condition. It doesn't matter if you are a novice or a professional carver; this is the book you should get and expand your woodcarving horizon!

https://www.amazon.com/dp/B084P6T7Q3

The Pyrography, Woodcarving and Leather Crafting Beginners Guide with Exercises: A Beginner Friendly 3 in 1 Manual with Instructions on Wood Burning, Leatherworking and Woodworking

The essential craft book for all time!

This is the ultimate pastime book for folks of all ages and genders, which will keep you busy at any time of the day. This book is a compilation of three of my books on crafting covering;

- **Pyrography (Wood Burning)**

- **Woodcarving**

- **Leather Crafting**

The crafts thoroughly explained in this book will go a long way in honing your crafting skills and take you away from that everyday routine while you spend quality time in your workshop.

"The Pyrography, Woodcarving and Leather Crafting Beginners Guide with Exercises" is packed full of invaluable lessons, hints and guides that will bring out the craftsman in you.

As well as helping you develop crafting skills, you will also learn the importance of patience, building a focused and mindful attitude that is devoid of disturbances that are all around us.

Are you a bit confused about how to go about starting your first project? With your tools on your workbench and this book in front of you, and your journey towards crafting that masterpiece will be the most fun trip you have ever embarked on.

With your aim to have a grasp on what pyrography, leather crafting and woodworking are all about, this book covers everything that you need to know and much more.

Within the pages of this amazing book, you will learn;

Simple practice projects with illustrations to develop your confidence levels

How to shade, write and apply outlines

Variety of woods, equipments, finishing and your work bench

Simply and thoroughly explained wood carving methods

Temperature settings in wood burning

Importance facts about leather

Knowing what type of burning nibs to use

Cutting and making patterns

Stamping

Stitching

Embossing

Gluing

Coloring

Finishing

Beveling

How to source and care for leather

Projects

And so much more!

No matter the skill, project, or ideas you want to implement on your wood or leather piece, you will find all that in this book and much more!

What are you waiting for? GRAB a COPY now!

https://www.amazon.com/dp/B08HTG62H7

Leather Crafting Beginner's Manual: A Step-by-Step Illustrated Guide with Basic Leatherworking Projects and Techniques

Explore the fantastic world of leather crafting that will give you joy for ages!

• Need to have manual for both beginners and experienced hands working with leather

• Detailed and well-explained facts about leather, tools, techniques, and projects to help you with leather crafting

• Become acquainted with the necessary methods through well-taught guides on the use of essential tools, leather preparation, and finishing.

• Understand and put to practice skills such as stitching, forming, braiding, molding, lacing and embossing

• Sequential photographic illustration of the different processes and tools

• Incredibly easy to craft projects for you!

Leather crafting is a timeless art that is not limited to any age bracket or skill level. If you are a pro in search of a brush-up material or a beginner needing proper grounding, Leather

Crafting for Beginner's is your go-to manual for a fun crafting experience.

Clayton M. Rines introduce you to the foundations of leather, its structure, types, preparation, how to use embossing tools, awls, cutters, stamps, etc. He gives essential hints on how to braid, stitch and craft primary, intermediary, and difficult leatherworks.

This book contains;

- Historical facts about leather

- Cutting and making patterns

- Stitching

- Stamping

- Gluing

- Embossing

- Beveling

- Coloring

- Finishing

- How to care and source for leather

- Projects

- And so much more!

No matter the skill, project, or ideas that you want to implement on your leather piece such as the making of a leather bracelet, cufflinks, pouches, passport cover, Leather Mason Jar Koozie, amazing scrap leather projects, etc., you will find all that in this book and much more!

Begin your leatherworking journey today with that can-do attitude.

CLICK the buy button now!

https://www.amazon.com/dp/Bo8KH3T1PS

About the Author

Clayton M. Rines is a techie who lives in and around gadgets. Knowing what makes devices all around us tick is his life ambition, and he is always on the lookout for new ideas to everyday technological problems. Bringing solutions to your gadget issues, giving opinions and tips on how to get the best out of your devices, and bringing to you excellent news gives him so much pleasure. He is a DIY expert, naturalist and animal lover.

Clayton is from Sacramento, California and enjoys globetrotting, savoring new experiences, enjoying new cultures.

Made in the USA
Columbia, SC
19 December 2023

d58e81b8-cb6f-43b7-a3ef-6faa0bd311e1R01